Instructor's Manual
to accompany

**Basic Contract Law
for Paralegals**

Third Edition

Jeffrey A. Helewitz
Adjunct Faculty, Paralegal Series
Adelphi University
Queens College
Baruch College
Marymount Manhattan College

Aspen Law and Business
Aspen Publishers, Inc.
Gaithersburg   New York

ISBN 0 - 7355 - 1986 - 2

Permissions
Aspen Law & Business
A Division of Aspen Publishers, Inc.
1185 Avenue of the Americas
New York, NY 10036

1 2 3 4 5

CONTENTS

Introduction

BASIC CONTRACT LAW FOR PARALEGALS, 3d ed. is designed to be used by all types of paralegal institutions. Regardless of whether a particular program has a specific course in contract law, or contract law is taught tangentially as a part of other curricula, BASIC CONTRACT LAW FOR PARALEGALS can be utilized either as a main text or as a supplement to other course material. Furthermore, the chapters have been designed so that the text can be used in courses covering an entire academic semester or any portion thereof.

BASIC CONTRACT LAW FOR PARALEGALS ,3d. ed. encompasses various methods of paralegal instruction. The book may be used as a primary text for teachers who favor a lecture-type approach to the subject. Also, each chapter contains full or abbreviated judicial decisions that highlight points discussed in the chapter and therefore can be used to teach the material using the Socratic method. Supplemental cases are suggested for outside reading by the students. Every chapter contains sample clauses that provide a practical approach to a discussion of contract law, drafting and analysis. Finally, exercise questions which appear at the end of each chapter provide an opportunity to highlight the chapter material, either as homework assignments or as the basis for classroom discussion.

Every chapter is designed in a similar format. The chapter starts with a basic overview of the material to be discussed. The Chapter Overview is designed as a prose synopsis of the basic legal principles and terminology of the chapter. Its purpose is to provide the student with the fundamental principles of the text and to prepare him or her for the fuller discussion that follows.

The main text of the chapter provides the student with basic concepts of contract law in a manner that is readily understandable by the paralegal. At this point in the text no reference is made to specific judicial decisions, primarily because paralegal students, as a general rule, find attempting to learn legal principles from case studies too complicated. However, every principle is highlighted with simple examples, all of which emanate from real life situations – either from relationships that have been reported in the newspapers and on television, actual judicial decisions, or day-to-day circumstances. These examples help clarify the primary principles and add some shading to the basic concepts.

Following the main text, every chapter includes a section on Sample Clauses. These clauses are presented to illustrate how the principles previously discussed may appear in actual contracts. For courses that focus on a practical, rather than theoretical, approach to the subject, this section can be used as the basis for drafting and interpreting simple contracts.

Every chapter has a Chapter Summary that not only reinforces the principles discussed, but also contains a Synopsis that the student can use as a basic outline during lectures, interlineating notes from the class in this portion of the text.

For those instructors who favor the case analysis method of instruction, every chapter has two Case Summaries followed by questions about the cases. These summaries can be used to demonstrate judicial interpretation of the contract principles discussed in the chapter, indicating how different factual situations influence the outcome. This section of the text introduces the cases with a brief statement indicating the purpose and importance of the case with respect to the preceding text. The selected cases come from all of the jurisdictions, and many are well known and notorious.

Every chapter concludes with Suggested Case References and Exercises. The Suggested Case References are introduced by raising questions that the judicial decision will answer and are intended to provide the student with outside, independent work. The Exercises raise questions that highlight the chapter material, and several ask for simple drafting of contractual provisions, similar to the work a paralegal might do for a law firm or corporation.

The only chapter in the book that deviates from the standard chapter format is Chapter 12, Drafting Simple Contracts. This chapter is designed specifically to give paralegal students a basic outline and structure for drafting and interpreting contracts. Few, if any, books on the market take such a detailed and specific approach to draftsmanship, and this chapter can be used as the core instructional tool for those programs that only introduce contract law peripherally to other courses.

The main text is followed by an Appendix containing 15 sample contracts that can be used as a research source by the student or as a teaching tool by the instructor by having the students criticize and rewrite the sample agreements. This provides an extremely practical approach to contract law, especially taken in conjunction with Chapter 12.

BASIC CONTRACT LAW FOR PARALEGALS, 3d ed. provides, in one format, a source for various methods of instruction and course work, and can be divided up by the instructor depending upon the needs of a particular program. For example, for those courses that are predominantly case oriented, the Case Summaries and Suggested Case References can be used exclusively, especially for a program that devotes a minimum amount of time to contract law. For a more practical approach, the Sample Clauses section in each chapter, taken in conjunction with Chapter 12, Drafting Simple Contracts, and the Appendix, provides an excellent basis for learning the material. And for those courses that have a more traditional approach, the basic text provides a simple and straightforward discussion of the law in a manner specifically designed to appeal to the paralegal student.

Sample Syllabi

The following suggested syllabi have been included in the Instructor's Manual in order to indicate how the text can be incorporated into various types of paralegal program schedules. The syllabi include a sixteen week program divided into two classes per week, a twelve week program with one longer class session each week, and finally, a short, four session practical course approach.

Sixteen Week Program

	Topic
1	General Introduction; Ch. 1: Overview of Contracts: General Overview
2	Ch. 1: Basic Requirements
3	Ch. 1: Classification of Contracts
4	Ch. 1: Case Analysis and Summary
5	Ch. 2: Offer: Definition, Essential Terms
6	Ch. 2: Essential Terms (cont.), Sample Offers
7	Ch. 2: Case Analysis
8	Ch. 3: Acceptance: Definition, Methods of Acceptance
9	Ch. 3: Termination of Acceptance
10	Ch. 3: Case Analysis
11	Ch. 4: Consideration: Defined
12	Ch. 4: Sufficiency, Promissory Estoppel
13	Ch. 4: Case Analysis
14	Ch. 5: Legality of Subject Matter and Contractual Capacity
15	Review
16	Mid-term Exam
17	Ch. 6: Contractual Intent: Fraud and Misrepresentation
18	Ch. 6: Duress, Mistake
19	Ch. 6: Case Analysis
20	Ch. 7: Contract Provisions: Statute of Frauds
21	Ch. 7: Covenants and Conditions, Rule of Construction
22	Ch. 7: Cases Analysis and Sample Drafting
23	Ch. 8: The Uniform Commercial Code: Art I
24	Ch. 8: Art. II
25	Ch. 8: Art. IX, Case Analysis
26	Ch. 9: Third Party Contracts: Third Party Beneficiary Contracts

Twelve Week Program

Four Session Practical Course

Session	Topic
1	Ch. 1: Overview of Contracts
2	Ch. 7: Contract Provisions
3	Ch. 12: Drafting Simple Contracts
4	Appendix: Analysis of Simple Contracts

Chapter 1
Overview of Contracts

The purpose of this chapter is to give the student an overview of all of contract law. It is an introduction to all of the topics that will be discussed in detail in the subsequent chapters and is intended merely as an introduction to the subject matter.

Every chapter starts with a Chapter Overview that directs the student to the most important matters that are going to be discussed in the remainder of the text. By having the overview, the student is given some familiarity with the subject matter before it is discussed in detail; because the material already has been presented, the complete chapter does not appear to be so formidable.

Section B, Basic Contract Requirements, highlights the six requirements to create a valid contract. Every statement of law is followed by one or more examples, giving practical meaning to the black letter law just presented. Every example comes from a real life situation, and several are taken from judicial decisions and notorious events. No reference is made to specific case law in the main body of the text because paralegal students, unlike law students, are not used to determining law from judicial opinions, and constant case references tend to confuse the students. However, specific cases are discussed at the end of each chapter so that the "case method, of instruction can be incorporated into the course. Classifications of Contracts, Section C, provides a menu of all possible configurations of contracts, classified by type of obligation, method of creation, form, timing, and enforceability. This section provides a good starting point for discussing the validity and enforceability of contractual agreements. Most lay persons believe that the only "real" contract is a written contract, and that all written contracts can be enforced. By analyzing the classifications given here, the student is exposed to a wider intellectual concept with respect to legal relationships. The examples also provide good points of discussion, especially with respect to unilateral versus bilateral contracts. The student now begins to realize that most of his or her day-to-day relationships involve some aspect of contract law.

The chapter continues with a section on Sample Clauses. These clauses highlight various ways in which the subject matter discussed in the chapter may appear in a real life situation. This section provides both a basis for a discussion of contract drafting and a discussion of how each clause fits into the material previously discussed. Every sample includes some analysis, which can be the focus of classroom discussion.

The Chapter Summary is divided into two main sections. The first section is a prose recapitulation of the material covered in the chapter. This recapitulation reinforces the material learned throughout the chapter and provides the student with a quick review. The second section is a Synopsis, which acts an outline of the text. Most paralegal students like to be given an outline of the course material, and BASIC CONTRACT LAW FOR PARALEGALS, 3d ed. provides such an outline. The outline can be used during the classroom discussion so that class notes can be interlineated with the Synopsis, giving the student the ability to listen to the lecture rather than taking notes all of the time.

The Chapter Summary is immediately followed by a mini-glossary , called Key Terms, which is a listing of the terms discussed in the chapter. Because precision of language is crucial to the practice of law, it is important that the students be able to use and define legal terms correctly. Not only does the Key Terms section provide a quick reference to the terminology, but it also acts as a review of the material presented, giving additional reinforcement of the knowledge gained.

The chapter includes five Exercises. Questions 1 and 4 let the student do some drafting of a simple contract. Questions 2 and 3 involve discussing some principles highlighted in the main part of the chapter. The last question is one that has no right or wrong answer but asks the student to expand the general principles of the chapter into the larger concept of proof. Students always want to know how something can be proven – this question gives them the opportunity to come to their own conclusions and exemplifies the importance of noting all circumstances surrounding the creation of a contractual relationship.

The chapter provides two Case Summaries, which are judicial decisions that are reprinted in whole or in part. These cases are introduced by a few sentences that indicate the important points discussed in the chapter that the cases highlight, and each case is followed by questions that can be used for a class discussion or as written homework assignments.

The *Duplex Envelope Co.* case is an older decision that provides several interesting points for discussion. The case concerns the requirements to create a valid contract.. This case provides a good opportunity to discuss drafting contracts which will be discussed in later chapters of the book.

The *Childs* case discusses express and implied contracts with respect to employment law. The court discusses the implications of tryout employment periods as creating a contract between the employer and the employee. This could have important ramifications to the student who may work for a large corporation or a governmental agency.

The Suggested Case References section of the chapter affords the student the opportunity to do some out of class library work, finding and analyzing additional judicial decisions. Each suggested case is introduced by a question that the student can answer by reading the material, or that the instructor can use to generate class discussion. The instructor can provide the case fact pattern to the student, see how the student would resolve the dispute, and then compare the student's resolution with the court's decision. These types of exercises are generally well received by students.

Chapter 2
Offer

This chapter concerns the starting point of every contractual relationship – the offer. It continues the overview of contracts discussed in Chapter 1 by providing a detailed analysis of the first requirement to the creation of a valid contract.

The Chapter Overview directs the student to the most important matters that will be discussed in the remainder of the text and prepares the student for the discussion by providing guidelines with respect to the main concepts of the chapter. The overview is followed by a brief discussion of the definition of an offer, picking up from what was introduced in Chapter 1.

Section C, Essential Terms of an Offer, details the four main terms required to appear in every offer: price, subject matter, parties, and timing of the performance. Many examples are provided from typical, day-to-day situations that highlight the material and can be used as the basis for classroom discussion, especially with respect to "reasonableness" as determined by the student and the courts. This section also introduces the student to the Uniform Commercial Code and indicates changes to common law that have bee effected by the Code in certain limited situations. Although the UCC is discussed in detail in Chapter 8, at this point it can provide a focus to a discussion of the difference between common law and statutory law and how they intertwine, especially with respect to contracts.

Section D, Sample Offers, indicates various methods whereby offers are expressed or enacted in everyday life. Each clause is followed by a short analysis, which can be used to start a discussion on draftsmanship or how the clauses indicated related to the material discussed in the text.

The Chapter summary is divided into two main sections. The first section is a prose recapitulation of the material contained in the chapter. This recapitulation reinforces the material learned throughout the chapter and provides the student with a quick review. The second section is a Synopsis, which acts as an outline of the chapter. Most paralegal students like to be given an outline of the course material, and BASIC CONTRACT LAW FOR PARALEGALS provides such an outline. The outline can be used during the class so that class notes can be interlineated with the Synopsis, giving the student the opportunity to listen to the lecture rather than taking notes all of the time.

The Chapter Summary is immediately followed by a mini-glossary containing all of the terms discussed in the chapter. Because precision in language is crucial to the practice of law, it is important that the student be able to use and define legal terms correctly. Not only does the Key Terms section provide a quick reference to the terminology, but it also acts as a review of the material discussed, providing additional reinforcement of the knowledge gained.

The chapter provides five Exercises. Questions 1 and 2 require the student to understand and argue both sides of the same situation, underscoring the point that one never knows which side a firm may be representing in a contractual dispute. Question 3 highlights the implication of the Uniform Commercial Code on contracts. Finally, Questions 4 and 5 require simple drafting that can be used to give the student a feel for the practical aspects of a contract law practice.

The chapter includes two Case Summaries that are intended to highlight some important concepts learned in the chapter and to afford the instructor the opportunity to teach by the case method. The cases are introduced by short sentences indicating how the cases relate to the chapter material, and each case is followed by several case discussion questions.

In *Alligood v. Proctor & Gamble Co.* the student is able to discover how the wording of a newspaper ad may be used to argue that the ad is either an offer or a bid to offer.

The *Rogus* case focuses on membership in a professional association creating a contractual relationship between the members. Because most students currently or will belong to a professional organization the classroom discussion could start with how these memberships affect everyday life. These discussions make contract law seem much more real and personal to the students, as opposed to the mere recitation of facts in a judicial decision.

The Case Summaries are followed by Suggested Case References. Each suggested case is introduced by questions that can be used for classroom discussion or as the basis of independent library work to be done by the student outside of the classroom setting. The cases can be assigned as homework or can be discussed in class with the instructor providing the facts of the case and asking the students to argue for the parties or to settle the dispute.

Chapter 3
Acceptance

The purpose of this chapter is to inform the student of the various methods of accepting an offer, and the requirements and ramifications incident thereto. The chapter begins with a Chapter Overview that presents a short summary of the material that will be detailed in the chapter. This preview allows the student to prepare for the material that will be presented by having the most important points highlighted beforehand.

The main text of the chapter starts with the Definition of Acceptance. This section is a natural progression of the first chapter in its discussion of the six requirements for the creation of a valid contract. This portion of the chapter discusses the implications of an offeree varying the terms of the offer or the offeree remaining silent and indicates who has the power to accept an offer. Discussion can usually be generated with respect to silence because most students have received various types of offers in the mail and can relate the text material to their own lives.

Section C, Methods of Acceptance, details the difference in the means of accepting bilateral and unilateral contracts and introduces the Mailbox Rule. With the various advances in technology since the formation of the Mailbox Rule, the effect of the Rule on modern means of transmission can be analyzed in the classroom

The next section of the chapter covers the termination of an offer, and presents the concept of "operation of law." Operation of law may be a new concept for most of the students, and examples can be discussed with respect to each of the methods highlighted in the text, especially with respect to supervening illegality.

This chapter is the only chapter that contains no Sample Clauses because of the Mirror Image Rule. This can be discussed in detail in class as a reinforcement of the concept of the effect of varying the terms of the offer.

The Chapter summary is divided into two main sections. The first section is a prose recapitulation of the material covered in the chapter and provides the student with a quick review. The second section is a synopsis that acts as an outline of the chapter material. Most paralegal students like to be given an outline of the course material, and BASIC CONTRACT LAW FOR PARALEGALS, 3d ed. provides such an outline. The outline can be used during the classroom discussion so that class notes can be interlineated with the synopsis, letting the student listen to the lecture rather than taking down notes as dictation.

The Chapter Summary is followed by a glossary of Key Terms that have been discussed in the chapter and can be used by the student to reinforce his or her recollection of the most important terms analyzed.

The chapter continues with five Exercise questions. Questions 1, 2, and 5 are general questions that require a basic understanding of the material contained in the chapter. Question 3 is an exercise in simple contract drafting in which the student is required to put some limitations on the ability of the offeree to accept. Question 4 is a theoretical question asking the student to argue the law presented in the text and to argue a proposition resolving the examples given in the text. By arguing opposite sides of the same set of facts, the student gets the perspective of what it is like to have a real client whose position may not always be the easily argued side of a controversy. These questions can be discussed in class or given as a written homework assignment. Question 4 also could be used for mock argument in the classroom.

Chapter 3 provides two Case Summaries that are intended to underscore the concepts of revocation of a unilateral order and a variation of the Mailbox Rule. The questions following the *Marchiondo* case provide the student with an opportunity to analyze the decision of the court, in comparison to materials presented in the text.

In the *University Emergency Medicine Foundation* case the student is presented with a situation involving a mailed notice of termination. This can generate a discussion of how particular facts can change a legal outcome. Also, the question following the case gives the student the chance to analyze a contract clause in the same manner that the court does, and to come up with his or her own conclusion.

The Suggested Case References highlight *Adams v. Lindsell*, the case that established the Mailbox Rule, and lets the student analyze the facts the court found determinative. This can be done in class or as a homework assignment. The second case provides an interesting factual situation that can be used to generate classroom discussion of unilateral contracts and the requirements with respect to a person's ability to accept an offer.

Chapter 4
Consideration

The purpose of this chapter is to illustrate legal consideration. Most students have no problem with the idea of consideration if the contract concerns physical property or money, but many are confused by the concept that consideration may be a detriment incurred at the request of the other contracting party.

The Chapter Overview, as with all the chapters, provides an introductory note with respect to the legal concepts that will be discussed in the body of the chapter. The purpose of the overview is to focus the student's mind on the legal principles involved with consideration and to highlight the material that will be detailed in the text.

Section B defines "consideration," both as a benefit conferred and a detriment incurred. This section has several examples of both categories of consideration, all taken from everyday life, and it would be helpful to have the student discuss the consideration he or she has given and received in his or her own contractual relationships. Many students fail to realize how many contracts they actually enter into each day.

Section C delineates the most common circumstances in which the courts have determined that no consideration exists. Probably the most difficult circumstance for the student to comprehend is an illusory promise. The chapter contains several examples of such situation, but the difference between illusory promises, gifts, and actual consideration should be stressed and discussed at this point.

The following section concerns the sufficiency of the consideration, and the difference between nominal and sham consideration. It is important to focus on the "legal" value of the consideration under the circumstances of the particular situation. Point out that the mere dollar value of the consideration may be irrelevant to its sufficiency. There are examples in this section underscoring this point.

Section E on Promissory Estoppel can be used to reinforce the material discussed with respect to illusory promises and gifts. The three historical examples of promissory estoppel are discussed in this section; the instructor may want to have the students come up with their own examples of promissory estoppel.

Special Agreements, Section F, gives examples of specific arrangements that are deemed enforceable even though they do not contain what would typically be considered legally sufficient consideration. This section can be used as a starting point for a discussion of drafting simple contracts because of the special situations involved.

The chapter continues with Sample Clauses. These clauses highlight sections of contracts that contain consideration provisions and are followed by a short analysis of the clause. As a practical exercise, the student can be asked to analyze the clause and then suggest changes for different situations. In this fashion he or she will get some practice in simple draftsmanship.

Following the Sample Clauses, the chapter has a Chapter Summary to reinforce all of the material discussed in the preceding sections. The prose portion of the summary can be used as a quick review and refresher for the chapter material, and the Synopsis, which ends this portion of the chapter, provides an outline for the student that can be used as the basis of his or her notes for this section of the course.

The Key Terms section provides a short glossary of all the terms introduced in the chapter. By having a glossary at the end of the chapter, the definitions are reinforced so that the student is comfortable using the terms in their proper legal context.

Chapter 4 also has five Exercise questions. Questions 1, 2, and 3 require the student to articulate and explain several of the concepts discussed in the chapter, whereas Question 4 and 5 require outside library work so the student becomes acquainted with some specific statutory contract law for a particular jurisdiction. These Exercises can be used as the focus for classroom discussion or assigned as homework.

Chapter 4 provides two Case Summaries that are intended to highlight the concepts discussed in the text. The cases are introduced by a short paragraph indicating which areas of consideration are discussed in the decisions. The cases can be used to stimulate classroom discussion, or as the basis of the case method to teaching the course.

The *Don King* case covers several areas of consideration and will be intriguing to the students because of the notoriety of the participants. The extract that appears is actually culled from three decisions decided in a row, all dealing with the same situation. The questions following this excerpt require the student not only to analyze the court decision, but also to formulate his or her own ideas about the fairness of certain contracts based on changing circumstances. It might be interesting to discuss the concept of breaching a contract in order to avoid its obligations – perhaps the detriment of the damages will be outweighed by the ability to negotiate a new contract.

The *Cohen* case provides an interesting nuance to the concept of consideration: the idea of a reporter's promise of confidentiality to a source being the consideration of the agreement between the reporter and the source. The case distinguishes between consideration and promissory estoppel, which will help reinforce the chapter discussion.

Following the Case Summaries, several cases are suggested for outside reading. Each case is introduced by a question that the judicial decision resolves. These questions can be used as the basis of in-class discussion, or the outside references can be assigned as homework, having the student focus on the answer to the questions asked.

Chapter 5
Legality of Subject Matter
and Contractual Capacity

Chapter 5 is a short chapter concerning two fairly straightforward areas of contract law: legality of the subject matter and contractual capacity.

The Chapter Overview provides a short introduction to the material to be covered and indicates the most important points that will be discussed thereby focusing the student's attention to the most crucial areas.

Section B differentiates between those acts that are *malum in se* and those that are *malum prohibitum*. For the most part, few students have any difficulty with these situations and it can be covered fairly quickly.

Section C discusses contractual capacity and, again, this area generally provides few problems for the students.

As with all of the chapters in the book, Chapter 5 includes a Chapter Summary and a section of Key Terms that correspond to the similar sections of the earlier chapters.

The chapter provides five Exercise problems. Questions 1 and 3 require the student to absorb and synthesize the material discussed in the chapter. Question 2 presents an opportunity for the student to discuss proving facts that are external to the written contract. Question 4, based on a true factual situation, asks the student to argue for and against a particular proposition, highlighting questions of legality and morality as well as statutory regulation of certain areas of life. This question could be used to create a "moot court" classroom exercise, with some students arguing each side and other students rendering the decision.

The key area of interest in this chapter is the section of Case Summaries. These cases were selected because of the unusual, interesting, and notorious aspects of the parties. Because the text material is fairly straightforward, the cases provide most of the real interest in this section.

The first case, *United States v . Yazell*, involves the marital status of a woman as determinative of her ability to contract. The questions provide an opportunity for the student to analyze social implications and their effect on contract law.

The *Matter of Baby M* is a very well known case, but only certain sections pertinent to a contract discussion have been reprinted in the text. The questions following this case present certain moral and ethical considerations with respect to contractual arrangements and focus on some problems of draftmanship. Based on the court decision, it might have been possible to reword the agreement between the parties so as to obtain a different judicial result. The student can test his or her own drafting skills by rewriting the contract according to the decision of the court.

The Suggested Case References introduce more questions with respect to capacity and morality. These cases can be read outside of class or introduced in the class to spur discussion of the area.

Chapter 6
Contractual Intent

The objective of this chapter is to introduce the concept that external events can have an effect on the validity and enforceability of a contractual relationship. Many students believe that if a contract exists on paper its terms are enforceable. This chapter provides the opportunity to discuss the idea that intent is an important factor in contracts, as well as other areas of law.

The chapter starts with a Chapter Overview that highlights the main areas that will be discussed in the text: fraud and misrepresentation; duress; and mistake. The most important points are previewed in order to focus the student's attention on the material that will follow.

Contractual intent is defined by explaining that subjective factors must be taken into consideration when interpreting the validity of a contractual agreement. Most of the book concerns that concept of "reasonableness" and objective interpretation, so this is a slightly new point to be considered by the student.

Section C, Fraud and Misrepresentation, indicates the five requisite elements of contractual fraud and contracts fraud with misrepresentation. The distinction between fraud and misrepresentation can provide the basis for classroom discussion on when misrepresentation becomes fraud, how fraud can be proven, and the potential criminal implications of fraudulent contractual situations. It is a good idea to reinforce the concept that a single factual circumstance may involve several areas of law – most students tend to categorize facts into only one area of legal concern.

The section on Duress includes a discussion of physical, economic, and mental duress, as well as contracts of adhesion. The two areas that usually cause problems for students are economic duress and contracts of adhesion. The classroom discussion can focus on proving the elements of duress in attempting to void a contract.

Section E, Mistake, is a good starting point for differentiating between objective and subjective factors and problems in draftsmanship and interpretation. Because paralegals are often called upon to draft initial versions of contracts, or to interpret existing documents, special attention can be drawn to mistakes and ambiguities in creating the terms of the contract.

The chapter continues with a Chapter Summary that provides a recapitulation of the material discussed in the body of the chapter. The summary acts as a quick review of the subject matter and as a reinforcement of the concepts learned. In addition, the Chapter Summary includes a Synopsis, which acts as an outline for the student that can be used as preparation for classroom lectures.

The section of Key Terms is, in fact, a mini-glossary of the terms used in the chapter. This section reinforces the legal terminology that is imperative for the paralegal to understand in order to function effectively in a work situation.

Chapter 6 provides five Exercise problems. Question 1 is a simple fact pattern based on the chapter material that can be discussed or argued for both sides. The last four questions all require the student to be able to synthesize and explain the concepts learned in the chapter.

Two Case Summaries are included as an exercise in case analysis and the case method of instruction. The cases are introduced by a brief paragraph that explains how the cases relate to the material contained in the chapter.

The first case, *Francois v Francois*, introduces the concept of contract law's impact on divorce and property settlement. The questions following this case focus on duress, fraud, and misrepresentation in a marital dispute and interpretation of a prenuptial agreement.

Brown v. L.V. marks 7 Sons, Co. involves an fraud in the procurement of a contract. The case also introduces some evidentiary issues involved in contract litigation.

The section of Case Summaries is followed by four Suggested Case References. These cases are introduced by questions that the cases resolve. The decisions can be assigned as homework for the students, or the questions themselves can be used as a starting point for classroom discussion.

Chapter 7
Contract Provisions

The objective of this chapter is to introduce the problems of drafting contracts. For those courses that focus exclusively on the practical aspects of a contract practice, this chapter, in conjunction with Chapters 8 and 12, can be used as a primary text for contract creation.

The chapter starts with a Chapter Overview that introduces the basic concepts that will be discussed and previews the most important aspects of the chapter. The overview affords the student the opportunity to become prepared for the text that follows.

The body of the text commences with a discussion of the Statute of Frauds. This section relates back to Chapter 1 by indicating that there are certain exceptions to the general rule that contracts may be either written or oral. A distinction should be made between validity and enforceability of oral contracts that come within the Statute; many students confuse the two concepts.

Sections C and D contrast Covenants with Conditions. This is an excellent opportunity to begin a classroom exercise in contract interpretation. Not only can the examples given internally in these sections be used, but also reference can be made to one or more contracts appearing in the Appendix. The student can be asked to go through a contract to identify covenants and conditions.

Court Doctrines, Section E, concentrates on the Rules of Construction and the Parol Evidence Rule, so that the student becomes aware of external factors that will influence the interpretation, and hence the creation, of contractual agreements.

Section F provides Sample Clauses, followed by a short analysis of each clause given. These samples, once again, can be used as the basis for a discussion of drafting appropriate contractual clauses to meet the specific needs of a given client.

The Chapter Summary provides a review of all the material discussed in the text in order to reinforce the knowledge gained. The summary also includes a Synopsis, or outline, of the material, which the student can use as a quick review and as the basis of classroom lecture notes.

Section H is a listing of Key Terms used in the chapter and should remind the student of and reinforce the precise meanings of the legal terminology incident to this material.

The chapter includes five Exercise problems. Questions 1, 4, and 5 involve understanding the chapter material and simple drafting of contract clauses to exemplify the concepts. Questions 2 and 3 only require a synthesis of the material without asking for any specific drafting.

Chapter 7 includes two Case Summaries that are introduced by a short paragraph highlighting the portion of the text covered by the judicial decisions. These Summaries can be used to generate a classroom exercise in case analysis.

The *Nestle Food Co.* case involves a restrictive covenant and its enforceability. The questions following the case focus on the factors the court uses to interpret the provisions of the contract in question and asks the student to rewrite the contract based on the court's findings.

The *Loyal Erector* case concerns the difference between a condition and a covenant, and the subsequent questions ask the student to do his or her own analysis of the facts presented and court's interpretation.

Section J provides Suggest Case References that can be used as a homework assignment or as the basis of a classroom discussion. Note that the third suggestion is to locate your own Statute of Frauds, a good practical exercise for the student.

Chapter 8
The Uniform Commercial Code

The purpose of this chapter is to detail very specific provisions of the Uniform Commercial Code that have a direct impact on contract law. The Chapter Overview indicates the three main areas of the Code that will be discussed in the chapter: Article I, General Provisions; Article II, Sales; and Article IX, Secured Transactions. This chapter deals directly with contract provisions and, therefore, provides a basis for exercises in contract drafting.

A General Background of the history of the Code is provided at the beginning of the chapter. The General Background specifies the state, as opposed to the federal, basis of the UCC. Many students who have heard of the Code assume it is a nationwide federal law, and this introduction is used to help direct the student to the version adopted in each particular jurisdiction.

The first article discussed, Article I, deals with the General Provisions of the Code and is used to establish the parameters of the basic obligations and rights imposed by the statute. Specific attention should be drawn to the provisions establishing good faith and custom and usage as a statutory, as opposed to common law, requirement.

The heart of this chapter really begins with the discussion of Article II, Sales. Because most commercial contracts are governed by UCC provisions, particular attention is drawn to the nature of contract covered by the Code. Good areas for discussion would be the difference between goods and service contracts, and the purpose and implication of warranties in creating contracts and instigating litigation. This last topic is further highlighted by the Case Summaries provided at the end of the chapter.

Specific contractual provisions dealing with the risk of loss and transference of title are detailed, and the specific remedies available under the UCC are discussed. These remedies should be borne in mind later on when discussing Chapter 11, Remedies, to see how the Code affects persons who come within its provisions and allows remedies that are different than those available under common law.

Article IX, Secured Transactions, highlights two important areas of paralegal work. First, the text discusses the requirement for creating a security interest, and attention should be drawn to drafting an appropriate security interest clause in contracts. Some examples are given here, later in the chapter, and in contracts appearing in the Appendix to the book. The chapter then goes on to discuss the problems of perfecting a security interest, and because paralegals are typically the ones who must arrange for the search and file for perfected interests, the practical implication of this section should be stressed. The instructor can also point out the use of services in searching and filing security interests.

Sample Clauses are provided that exemplify the text discussion, and each clause is followed by a short analysis. The student can discuss how these clauses can be incorporated into the body of a contract.

The Chapter Summary provides a quick review of all the material discussed in the chapter and is intended to reinforce the concepts learned. The summary also includes a Synopsis of the material in outline form, which can be used as a basis of lecture notes.

A section of Key Terms is included to reiterate the specific meanings of the terms used in the chapter. Especially with reference to the Code, where definitions are so important, special emphasis should be placed on this section. Additionally, it can be pointed out to the student that the easiest way to get a client out of a Code problem is to determine that the client's situation fails to meet the requisite definition as used by the Code.

Chapter 8 also has five Exercise problems. The first three questions involve a basic understanding of the chapter material. The fourth and fifth questions are of a more practical nature: finding your own state's offices for filing financing statements. This exercise gives practical experience to the student, both in contract work and basic research.

Two Case Summaries are reprinted for classroom discussion. The first case, *Hong v. Marriott Corp.*, is an amusing case that students enjoy because of its *obiter dicta*. The questions following *Hong* focus on the concept of warranties and why a plaintiff would attempt to find a breach of warranty. The second decision, *In re Peregrine Entertainment, Ltd.*, highlights the problems encountered in attempting to perfect a security interest in intellectual property. The case introduces the concept of intellectual property and the problems of conflicting statutory requirements. The questions that follow the case require the student to concentrate on client problem solving based on the judicial decision.

The Suggested Case References afford the student the opportunity to do some outside research into his or her own state's version of the UCC, and includes additional judicial analysis of warranties and security agreements. These cases can be assigned as homework or used as the basis of classroom discussion. The Suggested Case References also provide the opportunity for a take-home exam.

Chapter 9
Third Party Contracts

The purpose of this chapter is to alert the student to the fact that not all contracts actually impose duties and obligation on the contracting parties; there may be persons not originally party to the contract who wind up having enforceable contract rights and obligations.

The Chapter Overview gives a short outline of the different types of third party contracts that will be discussed in the chapter. The chapter deals specifically with three types of third party relationships: third party beneficiary contracts, assignments, and delegations. The overview indicates the basic differences between these types of situations.

The main text of the chapter commences with a discussion of Third Party Contracts generally, and then goes on to specify the difference between Third Party Creditor Beneficiary Contracts and Third Party Donee Beneficiary Contracts. Several examples are given of both types of situations, and the same factual circumstance is varied to provide the nuances that create the different types of contracts. In this manner the student can see how the same small group of people, by slight changes in the facts, can be involved in both types of third party beneficiary contracts.

Because these contractual situations are typically confusing for the student, a diagram has been provided indicating the differences in the two types of third party beneficiary contracts. The diagram can be used as the focal point of the classroom discussion, and thus the basis of the student's notes for this part of the course.

Section F discusses Assignments and differentiates assignments from third party beneficiary contracts. Usually, once the student has absorbed third party beneficiary contracts, both assignment and delegation appear fairly simple. Special attention should be placed on novations, which are discussed in this section, both for its impact on contractual obligations and as a practical alternative that may be used in negotiating and drafting contracts for clients.

Section G provides a brief discussion of delegation and highlights the types of obligations that may and may not be delegated, noting that the delegator never relinquishes liability for the contractual obligation.

Chapter 9 continues with some Sample Clauses that exemplify the text material, and each clause is followed by a brief analysis to help the student focus on the area of law specified by the sample clause.

The Chapter Summary is divided into two sections. The first section is a prose recapitulation of the material covered in the chapter. This recapitulation reinforces the material learned throughout the chapter and provides the student with a quick review. The second section is a Synopsis, which acts as an outline of the chapter. Most paralegal students like to be given outlines of the course material, and BASIC CONTRACT LAW FOR PARALEGALS, 3d ed. provides such an outline. This outline can be used during the classroom discussion so that class notes can be interlineated with the synopsis, giving the student the ability to listen rather than taking notes all of the time.

The Key Terms is a mini-glossary of all of the terms discussed in the chapter. This section provides both a quick reference to the important terminology of the text material, and a guideline for a quick review of the material discussed, reinforcing the knowledge gained.

The chapter provides five Exercise problems. Questions 1, 3, 4, and 5 all require the student to analyze and explain the material covered in the chapter.   Question 2 provides a drafting exercise for the student in the creation of third party beneficiary contracts.

Two Case Summaries are included in the chapter, introduced by a brief paragraph pointing out their importance with respect to the text material.

The first case, *Artist management Office, Inc.* is an intriguing situation involving entertainment law and third party contracts. The questions that follow the case introduce the concepts of quantum meruit and the difference between intended and incidental beneficiaries and encourage the student to review the analysis given by the court to arrive at his or he own conclusions.

The *Grossmire Estate* case highlights concepts of oral contracts, third party contracts, equitable remedies, and family factors that go into a court's reasoning. The questions following this case can be used to generate discussion with respect to the general application of society mores to judicial decisions.

Several Suggested Case references are included for outside work by the student. Each suggested case is introduced by a short sentence that highlights the important facts of the case or the effect of the case on the material discussed. The cases are taken from various jurisdictions to underscore the universality of basic contract principles.

Chapter 10
Discharge of Obligations

This chapter is a basic, straightforward chapter dealing with the various methods by which a contracting party may be discharged from his or her contractual obligations without being held in breach of contract. For the most part, students do not have much problem with this material and it can be covered fairly quickly.

The Chapter Overview provides a preview of the eight methods of discharge that will be discussed in the text. The overview if fairly brief and merely introduces the concepts that are going to be discussed.

Section B, Methods of Discharge, details all of the basic methods of discharging one's contractual obligations. The two areas that generally deserve more focus are the first method, Excuse of Conditions, because it raises many of the theories discussed in Chapter 7, and Frustration of Purpose, because it is unusual.

Sample Clauses provide some practical guidelines for incorporating the principles discussed in to drafting contract provisions. Each sample is followed by a short analysis indicating the purpose and usefulness of the clause.

The Chapter Summary is divided into two main sections. The first section is a prose recapitulation of the material covered in the chapter. This section reinforces the material learned throughout the chapter and provides the student with a quick review. The second section is the Synopsis, which acts as an outline of the material discussed and can be used as a quick reference or as the basis of classroom lecture notes.

The Key Terms section provides a glossary of all of the terms discussed in the chapter. This section forces the student to focus on the exact legal definition of the terms employed, a basic requirement for any form of legal work.

Five exercise problems continue this chapter. Questions 1, 3, and 4 ask the student to analyze the legal theories discussed in the chapter. Questions 2 and 5 provide the opportunity for the student to do some simple contract drafting based on the text material. These problems can be assigned as homework or could be the basis for exam questions.

Two Case Summaries are included so that some case analysis may be used as part of the classroom discussion. The first case, *Dunaj*, discusses whether a party may be discharged from a contract because its fulfillment has become overly expensive. This is an important point for discussion because many contracts turn out to be more expensive to fulfill than the party originally intended. The questions following the case deal with this point and ask the student to redraft the contract discussed in the case so as to avoid the lawsuit.

Broome Construction Co. concerns methods of rescinding a contract. The questions following the case highlight concepts of oral versus written contracts and the Parol Evidence Rule and ask the student to analyze the court's reasoning.

Several Suggested Case References are included in order to provide some out of class work for the student. Each suggested case is introduced by legal questions that the case attempts to answer. These questions focus the student in his or her reading of the cases and can be used for classroom discussion.

Chapter 11
Remedies

The chapter covers the different types of remedies available to persons who have been injured by a breach of contract. Usually, this is the first thing students want to know about the "What can I get?" aspect of law.

The chapter begins with a Chapter Overview to preview all of the types of remedies available to the injured party. The chapter is divided into four main areas: legal remedies, equitable remedies, waivers, and arbitration.

Section B, Legal Remedies, highlights the three main types of monetary awards granted in contractual disputes. The section on compensatory damages is exemplified by the factual situation of *Hawkins v. McGee*, the leading case in the area, as well as several examples from everyday situations. Punitive damages usually carries the most problems for the students, and the concept of the contractual breach coupled with some other fiduciary or moral violation should be emphasized. The section on consequential damages is highlighted by the famous case in the area, *Hadley v. Baxendale*. This section concludes with a discussion of some contractual provisions that can affect the amount of the damages awarded to the parties-liquidated damages and limitation of damages clauses.

Equitable Remedies, Section C, details the four main types of nonmonetary awards: injunctions (including TROs), specific performance, rescission and restitution, and reformation. Each of these subjects is exemplified by factual situations taken from everyday life, and examples discussed previously in the book. The last group of equitable remedies, the quasi-contractual remedies, is designed to reiterate the subjects and examples discussed in the beginning of the book. In this fashion the entire text is brought full circle.

Section D, Waivers and Their Effect, concentrates on contractual clauses and how waivers may affect the ability to sue and/or recover from a contractual breach. This section, in conjunction with the previous section on liquidated damages, can be used to focus on the problems and consequences of drafting contractual provisions.

The main text of the chapter concludes with a discussion of arbitration and its effect on damages. This section provides a good opportunity to discuss alternatives to litigation of contractual disputes, such as mediation, settlement, and the like, thereby demonstrating a practical aspect of a contractual practice.

Section F, Sample Clauses, includes several examples of remedy clauses, followed by a brief analysis of the provision and its effect. Once again, this can present an opportunity to discuss the problems of contract drafting.

The Chapter Summary is divided into two main sections. The first provides a quick prose review of the subjects covered in the chapter in order to reinforce the material learned. The second section, the Synopsis, is an outline of the chapter material that can be used as the focus of the classroom lecture and lecture notes.

The Key Terms section is a mini-glossary of all the terms used in the chapter. By reinforcing the terminology, the student becomes more conversant and comfortable with legal phraseology, an important aspect of legal practice.

Chapter 11 provides five Exercises to stimulate analysis of the text material. Questions 1, 3, and 5 require an understanding of the basic material discussed in the chapter. Questions 2 and 4 involve the student in persuasive argument, asking him or her to argue a particular point of law; this can serve as a practical beginning to drafting simple memoranda of law.

Two Case Summaries are included, dealing with specific performance and exemplary damages. The *Guard* case concerns specific performance, and the questions following the summary focus on when a party may seek specific performance and the validity of granting such relief. The *Goodyear* case presents the problems that are associated with seeking punitive damages, and is followed by a series of questions that ask the student to analyze the entire arrangement that existed between the parties in the case.

For Suggested Case References are included and demonstrate how courts tackle the different types of contractual remedies. These cases can be assigned as outside reading or used as the basis of classroom discussion or exams.

52

Chapter 12
Drafting Simple Contracts

This is the most practical chapter of the entire text. The purpose and objective of this chapter is to introduce the paralegal to drafting simple contracts. Legal assistants are often called upon to draft contracts but generally are given no guidance with respect to how to go about the task. This chapter provides the guidance.

Section B, Checklist of Clauses, discussed 17 basic types of clauses that, when put together, create a contract. Each of the clauses is exemplified and includes a discussion of the clause and its purpose in the contract. The classroom discussion can focus on each of the sample clauses, what is good and/or bad about them, and how they could be changed to meet the specifics of a particular client.

Section C provides a summary of the clauses discussed in the text, and a quick review of the best methods of creating a contract.

Chapter 12 concludes with four simple Exercises that involve the student in actual drafting and contract interpretation. These Exercises can be done in conjunction with a review of the sample contracts that appear in the Appendix. By using the sample given in the text of the chapter, the contracts appearing in the Appendix, and the Exercises, the student is afforded an excellent opportunity to get some practical experience in drawing up a simple contract. This aspect of the book is unique to BASIC CONTRACT LAW FOR PARALEGALS, 3d ed. and is the heart of the entire work.

SAMPLE EXAM QUESTIONS

This section is included in the Instructor's Manual in order to provide sample exam questions that can be used to reinforce the material contained in the main text. The sample questions are arranged into the following areas:

I.   Terms to Identify and/or Define

II.   True/False

III.   Short Answer

IV.   Essays

V.   Multiple Choice

I.   Terms to Identify and/or Define

Chapter One

1.   BILATERAL CONTRACT: A promise for a promise.

2.   IMPLIED-IN-FACT CONTRACT: A contract in which the promises of the parties are inferred from their actions as opposed to specific words.

3.   OPERATION OF LAW: A manner in which rights and obligations devolve on a person without the act or cooperation of the party himself or herself.

4.   PROMISOR: The one who gives consideration in a bilateral contract.

5.   UNILATERAL CONTRACT: A promise for an act.

6.   VOIDABLE CONTRACT: A contract that one party may avoid at his or her option without being in breach of contract.

Chapter Two

7.   OFFER: A proposition made by one party to another, manifesting a present intention to enter into a valid contract and creating a power in the other person to create a valid contract by making an appropriate acceptance.

8.   OUTPUT CONTRACT: An agreement whereby one party agrees to buy or sell all the goods produced by the other party.

Chapter Three

9.   ACCEPTANCE: Manifestation of assent in the manner requested or authorized by the offeror.

10.   MAILBOX RULE: The acceptance of a bilateral contract is effective when properly dispatched by an authorized means of communication.

Chapter Four

11. CONSIDERATION: A benefit conferred or a detriment incurred; a basic requirement of every valid contract.

12. LEGAL DUTY RULE: A promise to do what one is already legally bound to do is not consideration.

13. MUTUALITY OF CONSIDERATION: The bargain element of the contract; that each side must give and receive something of legal value.

14. PROMISSORY ESTOPPEL: Doctrine in which promises not supported by consideration are given enforceability if the promisee had detrimentally relied on the promises.

Chapter Five

15. CONTRACTUAL CAPACITY: The legal ability to enter into a contractual relationship.

16. STATUTE OF FRAUDS: Statute mandating that certain contracts must be in writing to be enforceable.

17. UNDUE INFLUENCE: Mental duress by a person in a close and particular relationship to the innocent party.

Chapter Six

18. FRAUD: A misrepresentation of a material fact made with the intent to deceive, relied upon by the other party to his or her detriment.

19. MISREPRESENTATION: Mistakes of a material fact relied upon by the other party to his or her detriment; no intent to defraud.

20.   UNILATERAL MISTAKE: Misconception of the subject matter of a contract by only one party to the contract; may be enforceable.

Chapter Seven

21.   CONDITION PRECEDENT: Fact or event that creates an absolute duty to perform.

22.   CONVENANT: An absolute, unconditional promise to perform.

23.   GUARANTEE: Promise to answer for the debts of another; must be in writing.

24.   PAROL EVIDENCE RULE: Oral testimony may not be used to vary the terms of a writing.

25.   RULES OF CONSTRUCTION: Guidelines used by the courts to interpret contractual provisions.

Chapter Eight

26.   COLLATERAL: Property subject of a security agreement under Article IX of the UCC.

27.   EXPRESS WARRANTY: A guarantee created by words or conduct of the seller.

28.   FINANCING STATEMENT:Document filed in government office to protect a security interest under Article IX of the UCC.

29.   SECURED TRANSACTION: Any transaction, regardless of form, that intends to create a security interest in personal property or fixtures.

30.   SHIPMENT CONTRACT: Agreement whereby risk passes from seller to buyer when goods are transported by a third person under Article II of the UCC.

31. UNIFORM COMMERCIAL CODE (UCC): Statutory enactment codifying certain areas of contract law, specifically with respect to sales contracts and security agreements.

32. WARRANTY: Guarantee made by the manufacturer or seller with respect to the quality, quantity, and type of good being sold.

Chapter Nine

33. ACCORD AND SATISFACTION: A special agreement in which the parties to disputed contract agree to new terms in exchange for forebearing to sue under the original agreement.

34. ASSIGNMENT: Transference of contractual rights by the promisee to a third party.

35. NOVATION: Substitution of a party to a contract-novated person takes overall rights and obligation under the contract.

36. REAL PARTY IN INTEREST: Person with enforceable contractual rights.

37. THIRD PARTY CREDITOR BENEFICIARY: Person who receives the benefit of a contract in order to extinguish a debt owed to him or her by the promisee.

Chapter Ten

38. BREACH OF CONTRACT: Failure of a promisor to fulfill a contractual obligation.

39. DIVISIBLE CONTRACT: Contract capable of being broken down into several equal agreements.

40. RELEASE: Contract relieving the promisor from an obligation under an existing contract.

41. TENDER PERFORMANCE: Being ready, willing, and able to perform.

Chapter Eleven

42. COMPENSATORY DAMAGES: Standard measure of damages, puts injured party in the same position he or she would have been in had the contract been fulfilled.

43. EQUITY: The branch of the legal system that deals with fairness and mercy.

44. EXEMPLARY DAMAGES: Additional monetary award designed to punish the breaching party.

45. INJUNCTION: Court order to stop engaging in a specific action.

46. LIMITATION OF DAMAGES: A contractual provision placing a ceiling on the amount of potential liability for breach of contract.

47. MITIGATION OF DAMAGES: Duty imposed on injured party to lessen, by reasonable means, the breaching party's liability.

48. QUANTUM MERUIT: Quasi-contractual aware; value of the service performed.

49. SPECIFIC PERFORMANCE: Court order to perform contractual promises.

50. WAIVER: Forgiveness of a contractual obligation.

II. TRUE/FALSE

Chapter One

1.   All contracts are considered bilateral under the law.

        FALSE

2.   Contracts inferred by the acts of the parties are known as quasi-contracts.

        FALSE

3.   A contract may be both valid and unenforceable.

        TRUE

4.   A formal contract is a written contract.

        FALSE

5.   Silence is acceptance of an implied-in-fact offer.

        TRUE

Chapter Two

6.   Time is an essential term of an offer.

        TRUE

7.   A court of law never implies terms that the parties have imperfectly covered.

        TRUE

Chapter Three

8.   A contract will be enforced even though one party has a unilateral right to decide

        the nature of the contractual performance.

        FALSE

9.

10. A unilateral contract can never be accepted by words.

    TRUE

11. Anyone who knows of an offer may accept it.

    FALSE

12. The Mailbox Rule determines the timing of the acceptance of a bilateral contract.

    TRUE

13. An offeree of a unilateral contract never has to notify the offeror of his or her

    acceptance.

    FALSE

Chapter Four

14. Consideration is the bargain aspect of the contract.

    TRUE

15. An offer may always be revoked by the offeror before acceptance by the offeree.

    FALSE

16. Lapse of time can act to terminate an offer.

    TRUE

17. A rejection is only effective on receipt by the offeror.

    TRUE

18. Moral consideration may be legally sufficient to create a contract.

    FALSE

19. Promissory estoppel is an example of contractual consideration.

    FALSE

20. The monetary value of the consideration is determinative of its legal value.

FALSE

21. Guarantees require no separate consideration.

TRUE

Chapter Five

22. A minor may avoid all contracts entered into upon reaching his or her majority.

FALSE

23. Contracts deemed *malum in se* are totally unenforceable.

TRUE

24. Violating a state usury law is *malum prohibitum.*

TRUE

25. Fraudulently inducing a person to enter into a contract is prohibited by the Statute of Frauds.

FALSE

Chapter Six

26. If both parties to a contract are unaware of an ambiguity in the terms, the contract will be enforced according to what both think.

TRUE

27. The difference between fraud and negligent misrepresentation is the intent of the parties.

TRUE

28. Contracts of adhesion are examples of contracts induced by duress.

TRUE

Chapter Seven

29.   Parol evidence may be used to explain the terms of a written contract.

FALSE

30.   A condition is an absolute duty to perform

FALSE

31.   Every contract must contain at least one covenant.

TRUE

32.   Constructive conditions are the same as implied-in-law conditions.

TRUE

Chapter Eight

33.   The Uniform Commercial Code covers contract for the sale of goods and services.

FALSE

34.   A security agreement may be filed as a financing statement.

TRUE

35.   The party who has the risk of loss of the goods in a sales contract has the right to insure the goods.

TRUE

36.   The UCC establishes a statutory standard of custom and usage for interpreting contracts.

TRUE

37.   The Uniform Commercial Code is a federal statute.

FALSE

38. A hobbyist may be considered a merchant under the UCC.

    TRUE

39. Replevin is a contractual remedy available under the UCC

    TRUE

40. All contracts are assignable.

    FALSE

Chapter Nine

41. A Third Party Creditor Beneficiary can sue the promisor of the contract for

    violating contract law.

    TRUE

42. Assignment only covers rights, not duties.

    TRUE

43. A Third Party Creditor Beneficiary's rights vest on his or her knowing of the

    contract.

    FALSE

44. The purpose of the third party beneficiary contract is to benefit a person not a

    party to the contract.

    TRUE

45. Novation is another term for assignment of rights.

    FALSE

Chapter Ten

46.   Partial performance never discharges a party from his or her duty of full

performance under a contract.

FALSE

Chapter Eleven

47.   An injured party has a duty to mitigate the damages the breaching party caused.

TRUE

48.   Consequential damages are usually available to an injured party.

FALSE

49.   Equitable remedies never include monetary awards.

FALSE

50.   Arbital awards can be appealed.

FALSE

51.   The standard measure for contractual damages is known as compensatory

damages.

TRUE

III. SHORT ANSWER

Chapter One

1. What are the six requirements to create a valid contract?

   Offer, acceptance, consideration, capacity, legality, and intent.

2. Exemplify an implied-in-fact contract

   Auctioneer, doctor's visit, and the like.

3. Explain the difference between a void contract and unenforceable contract.

   Void: never existed

   Unenforceable: valid but not legally capable of being performed.

4. When is a contract executory?

   When there are still promises or duties to be carried out.

5. Give two examples of a formal contract.

   Guarantee, charitable subscription.

6. Are voidable contracts enforceable?

   Only at the option of the party who can avoid the contract.

Chapter Two

7. What are the elements of every valid offer?

   1. Manifestation of present contractual intent;

   2. Certainty and definiteness of the terms; and

   3. Communication to the offeree.

8. What are the four essential terms of a valid offer?

   Parties, subject matter, time, and price.

9. How does the UCC affect the requirements of a valid offer?

More leeway given to merchants; no need to have all of the terms spelled out.

[Question could also apply to Chapter 8]

10. What is an output contract?

A contract in which one party agrees to purchase all products produced by the other party.

11. How can illusory promises become enforceable and binding?

By the act of the parties creating definiteness in the terms.

12. When does the offeror of a unilateral contract lose his or her ability to revoke?

After the offeree has made a substantial beginning on the requested performance.

Chapter Three

13. How does the Mailbox Rule affect rejections of offers?

Rejection is effective when received, acceptance when mailed-contract depends on the expectations of the offeror.

14. How can an offer be terminated?

Operation of law or act of the parties.

Chapter Four

15. What are the essential factors for contractual consideration?

Must be bargained for and have legal value.

16. What is meant by the "sufficiency of the consideration"?

Legal detriment or legal benefit.

Chapter Five

17.   What is contractual capacity?

Being over the age of consent, not being under the influence of drugs or alcohol, and understanding the nature of the contract.

Chapter Six

18.   What are the five elements of contractual fraud?

Misrepresentation

Of a material fact

With intent to deceive

Relied upon by the other party

To his or her detriment.

19.   Give an example of mental duress.

Threatening to injure a person's relative to induce signing a contract.

Chapter Seven

20.   What is a Rule of Construction?

A court doctrine used to interpret contract provisions.

21.   What is a condition?

Act or event, the happening or non-happening of which creates or extinguishes an absolute duty to perform.

22.   How are conditions classified with respect to time?

Precedent, subsequent, and concurrent.

23.   How does the Statute of Frauds influence the creation of contracts?

Requires certain contracts be in writing to be enforceable.

24. What are the exceptions to the Parol Evidence Rule?

To show failure of consideration

To show fraud or duress

To prove a collateral oral contract

To explain ambiguities.

Chapter Eight

25. What is the objective of the Uniform Commercial Code?

To promote commerce and uniformity among the states with respect to commercial transactions.

26. What types of contracts are covered by Article II of Uniform Commercial Code?

Sales of goods between merchants, valued at over $500, and lease of good.

27. What is a warranty, and what types of warranties are covered by the UCC?

A warranty is a guarantee: express, implied, and title.

28. How are express warranties created?

By manifestation of the seller: promises, samples, and descriptions.

29. What is meant by the attachment of a security interest?

The timing element of rights vesting.

30. What are the three requirements to create a security interest?

Security agreement, attachment, and perfection.

31. Explain the difference between cover and replevin.

Cover: goods in substitution.

Replevin: Reclaim rejected goods if cover isn't available.

32. Discuss several types of contract provisions dealing with the risk of loss occasioned by the sale of goods.

COD, FAS, FAB, consignment, and the like.

Chapter Nine

33. Give an example of a third party donee beneficiary contract.

Life insurance policy.

34. What contracts cannot be assigned?

Personal confidence, personal services, materially change duty of other party, and contract provision prohibiting assignment.

35. What is the effect of a token chose on a gratuitous assignment?

Makes the assignment irrevocable.

36. What duties may be delegated?

Non-personal duties.

37. Who can a third party creditor beneficiary sue if the contract is breached?

Either the promissor or his or her original creditor.

38. What is a novation?

A substitution of parties in a contract.

Chapter Ten

39. What is the consideration for an accord and satisfaction?

Both sides refrain from enforcing the original contract in a court of law.

40. What is the effect of a minor breach of contract?

Gives rise to an immediate cause of action for damages for that breach but not for the entire contract.

41. What factors determine whether a breach is material or minor?

    Intent; degree of hardship; extent of injury; extent to which breach can be remedied; and the like.

42. Are all contracts divisible?

    No.

43. Give an example of frustration of purpose.

    The Coronation Cases.

Chapter Eleven

44. What is the effect of a waiver on a breach of contract?

    Waiving party loses the ability to sue for that breach.

45. What is the difference between a TRO and an injunction?

    TRO is temporary; injunction is more or less permanent.

46. What are the quasi-contractual remedies?

    Quantum meruit and quantum valebant.

47. When are consequential damages permitted?

    When breaching party was made aware of special damages that would be suffered in case of breach before contract was entered into.

48. What are some alternatives to litigating a breach of contract?

    Arbitration, mediation, accord and satisfaction, recision and restitution, and the like.

49. How do exemplary damages differ from punitive damages?

    They don't – they are the same.

50.   What is the purpose of compensatory damages?

To put the injured party in the same position he or she would have been in had the

contract been fulfilled.

IV. Essays

1. Discuss in detail the method of creating and perfecting a valid security interest under Article IX of the Uniform Commercial Code.

2. Discuss in detail the clauses that should appear in a valid contract.

3. Analyze the Equipment Lease Agreement that appears in the Appendix of the text.

4. Discuss in detail all of the information you would want to get from a client before drafting an initial contract.

5. Discuss in detail the different requirements to create and modify a contract under the common law and the UCC.

V. Multiple Choice

Chapter One

1. A promise for a promise is an example of:

    A. A bilateral contract*

    B. A unilateral contract

    C. A formal contract

    D. An executory contract

2. A contract that one party may avoid with being in breach is

    A. Void

    B. Valid

    C. Voidable*

    D. Executory

3. All written contracts are

    A. Formal

    B. Valid

    C. Bilateral* [*could also be tested with Chapter 4*]

    D. Executed

Chapter Two

4. A non-essential term of an offer is

    A. Writing*

    B. Parties

    C. Price

    D. Subject Matter

5. If a contract term is ambiguous the contract is

    A. Probably void

    B. Probably enforceable*

    C. Probably unconscionable

    D. Probably unenforceable

6. An output contract is

    A. Illusory

    B. Unconscionable

    C. Voidable

    D. None of the above*

7. One party's unlimited right to decide the nature of the contractual performance is

    A. A quasi contract

    B. Illusory*

    C. Promissory estoppel

    D. None of the above

8.   An essential element of an offer is

   A.   Manifestation of present intent

   B.   Communication to the offeree

   C.   Certainty of the terms

   D.   All of the above*

9.   When one party has subjective control of the contract terms, the contract is

   A.   Void

   B.   Illusory*

   C.   An example of promissory estoppel

   D.   A quasi-contract

Chapter Three

10.   The person who can accept an offer is known as

   A.   The acceptor

   B.   The offeror

   C.   The assignee

   D.   The offeree*

Chapter Four

11.   *Caveat Venditor* means

     A.   Violating statutory law

     B.   Violating common law

     C.   Let the buyer beware

     D.   Let the seller beware*

12.   An example of valid consideration is

     A.   Past gifts

     B.   Moral obligations

     C.   Property of nominal value

     D.   None of the above*

13.   The bargain element of a contract is

     A.   The price

     B.   The offer

     C.   The consideration*

     D.   The intent

14.   To be deemed sufficient, the consideration of a contract must

     A.   Have monetary value

     B.   Be fair

     C.   Have legal value*

     D.   Be a moral obligation

Chapter Five

15. An example of lack of contractual capacity is

    A. A minor

    B. A drunk

    C. A person on drugs

    D. All of the above*

16. An example of a contract *malum se* is

    A. A contract in restraint of trade*

    B. A contract that is usurious

    C. A contract for gambling

    D. A contract that violates the Statute of Frauds

17. "Necessaries" do not include

    A. Transportation*

    B. Education

    C. Insurance

    D. Medical Care

18.   The Statute of Frauds

    A.   Is concerned with misrepresentation

    B.   Is concerned with perjury*

    C.   Is a common law doctrine

    D.   Is a federal standard

19.   Court doctrines used to interpret contracts are

    A.   Precedents

    B.   Statutory regulations

    C.   Stare decisis

    D.   Rules of construction*

20.   The Parol Evidence Rule prohibits oral testimony that

    A.   Shows failure of consideration

    B.   Explains ambiguities

    C.   Shows fraud

    D.   Varies the terms*

21.   The difference between fraud and misrepresentation is the element of

    A.   Intent*

    B.   Detriment

    C.   Materiality

    D.   Believability

Chapter Seven

22. An absolute promise to perform is a

    A.   Condition precedent

    B.   Contract

    C.   Covenant*

    D.   Condition

23. A contract clause conditioned on time may be an example of

    A.   An express condition

    B.   A condition precedent*

    C.   An implied condition

    D.   A covenant

Chapter Eight

24. To perfect a valid security interest under the UCC you do not need

    A.   Lien*

    B.   Attachment

    C.   Possession

    D.   Filing

25. An example of a destination contract under the UCC is

    A.   FAS (Vessel)

    B.   FOB (Carrier)

    C.   CIF

    D.   None of the above*

26. A seller under Article II of the UCC may be awarded replevin

    A.   Sometimes

    B.   Always

    C.   Usually

    D.   None of the above*

27. The Uniform Commercial Code is

    A.   A State law governing commerce*

    B.   A federal law governing commerce

    C.   An international law governing commerce

    D.   A model act

28. The person with the highest priority in a secured transaction is the one who

    A.   Attached first

    B.   Has a purchase money security interest*

    C.   Filed first

    D.   Has a floating lien

29.	Under the UCC the parties to the transaction

    A.	Are bound by the UCC

    B.	Are governed by state law

    C.	May vary the terms of their agreement from UCC rules*

    D.	Are governed by objective standards

30.	A guarantee to transfer rights to goods is

    A.	An express warranty

    B.	A warranty of title*

    C.	An implied warranty

    D.	A warranty of enforceability

31.	The UCC is

    A.	Concerned with the sale of goods valued at over $500*

    B.	Concerned with all goods

    C.	Concerned with service contracts

    D.	No concerned with leases

32.	Article IX of the UCC covers

    A.	Real estate

    B.	Copyrights

    C.	Garnishments

    D.	Fixtures*

33.   Under the UCC a merchant is

    A.   A salesman

    B.   A retailer*

    C.   An inventor

    D.   A Venetian

34.   In a sales contract, when the seller bears no risk of loss it is a

    A.   Destination contract

    B.   Consignment contract*

    C.   Special shipment contract

    D.   COD

35.   Under Article II of the UCC a seller may not

    A.   Withhold delivery

    B.   Replevy the goods*

    C.   Stop delivery in transit

    D.   Sell the goods

Chapter Nine

36.   An assignment of personal services is

    A.   Illegal

    B.   Generally permitted

    C.   Permitted with all the parties' consent*

    D.   Is never permitted

37.   Except for third party contracts, contracts always have only two parties.

        A.   Always true

        B.   Never true

        C.   Sometimes true

        D.   None of the above*

38.   Selling your textbook to pay off a student loan is

        A.   A third party creditor beneficiary contract*

        B.   Foolish

        C.   A third party donee beneficiary contract

        D.   An assignment

39.   A novation is an example of

        A.   A delegation

        B.   A third party beneficiary contract

        C.   A license

        D.   An assignment*

40.   A gratuitous assignment does not become irrevocable by

        A.   A writing

        B.   A token chose

        C.   A promise*

        D.   A novation

Chapter Ten

41. A contract terminating because of the destruction of the subject matter is an example of

    A. A Rule of Construction

    B. A voidable interest

    C. The operation of law*

    D. A supervening illegality

42. A person may be discharged from his or her contractual obligations by

    A. Insubstantial performance

    B. Complete performance

    C. Tendering performance

    D. All of the above*

43. The Coronation Cases are examples of

    A. Discharge by impossibility of performance

    B. Discharge by illness

    C. Discharge by frustration of purpose*

    D. Discharge by agreement

44. A supervening illegality

    A.   Voids the contract

    B.   Makes the contract unenforceable*

    C.   Has no effect on the contract

    D.   Makes the contract voidable

45. A method of avoiding litigation for a breach of contract is

    A.   A waiver

    B.   Arbitration

    C.   Accord and satisfaction

    D.   All of the above*

46. An example of excuse of conditions is

    A.   Voluntary disablement

    B.   Insolvency

    C.   Anticipatory breach

    D.   All of the above*

47. The Statute of Frauds does not cover

    A.   Contracts in consideration of marriage

    B.   Contracts for the sale of realty

    C.   Guarantees

    D.   Contracts to be performed within one year*

Chapter Eleven

48. *Quantum Meruit* is an example of

    A.   Quasi-contract

    B.   Equitable remedies*

    C.   Legal remedies

    D.   Promissory estoppel

49. A contractual clause establishing an amount of prospective damages for breach is

    A.   Mitigation of damages

    B.   Liquidated damages*

    C.   Against the law

    D.   Limitation of damages

50. An example of an equitable remedy is

    A.   Exemplary damages

    B.   Waivers

    C.   Consequential damages

    D.   None of the above*

SUPPLEMENTAL CASES

The following cases are included for those teachers who wish to utilize more cases for a case method approach to teaching the course.

<u>Brooke Shields v. Garry Gross</u>
58 N.Y.2d 338 (1983)

The issue on this appeal is whether an infant model may disaffirm a prior unrestricted consent executed on her behalf by her parent and maintain an action pursuant to section 51 of the Civil Rights Law against her photographer for republication of photographs of her. We hold that she may not.

Plaintiff is now a well-known actress. For many years prior to these events she had been a child model and in 1975, when she was 10 years of age, she obtained several modeling jobs with defendant through her agent, the Ford Model Agency. One of the jobs, a series of photographs to be financed by Playboy Press, required plaintiff to pose nude in a bathtub. It was intended that these photos would be used in a publication entitled "Portfolio 8" (later renamed "Sugar and Spice"). Before the photographic sessions, plaintiff's mother and legal guardian, Teri Shields, executed two consents in favor of defendant. After the pictures were taken, they were used not only in "Sugar and Spice" but also, to the knowledge of plaintiff and her mother, in other publications and in a display of larger-than-life photo enlargements in the windows of a store on Fifth Avenue in New York City. Indeed, plaintiff subsequently used the photos in a book that she published about herself and to do so her mother obtained an authorization from defendant to use them. Overthe years defendant has also photographed plaintiff for Penthouse Magazine, New York Magazine and for advertising by the Courtauldts and Avon companies.

In 1980 plaintiff learned that several of the 1975 photographs had appeared in a French magazine called "Photo" and, disturbed by that publication and by information that defendant intended others, she attempted to buy the negatives. In 1981, she commenced this action in tort and contract seeking compensatory and punitive damages and an injunction permanently enjoining defendant from any further use of the photographs. Special Term granted plaintiff a preliminary injunction. Although it determined that as a general proposition consents given by a parent pursuant to section 51 barred the infant's action, it found that plaintiff's claim that the consents were invalid or restricted the use of the photographs by Playboy Press presented questions of fact. After a nonjury trial the court ruled that the consents were unrestricted as to time and use and it therefore dismissed plaintiff's complaint. In doing so, however, it granted plaintiff limited relief. On defendant's stipulation it permanently enjoined defendant from using the photographs in "pornographic magazines or publications whose appeal is of a predominantly prurient nature" and it charged him with the duty of policing their use. The Appellate Division, by a divided court, modified the judgment on the law and granted plaintiff a permanent injunction enjoining defendant from using the pictures for purposes of advertising or trade. Two Justices voted for the result believing that plaintiff possessed a common-law right to disaffirm the consent given defendant by her parent. Justice Kupferman concurred, believing that in addition to the common-law right, the consents were governed by section 3-105 of the General Obligations Law and therefore could be interpreted to have expired after three years. Justice Asch also concurred in the result but on other grounds. He construed the transaction as a sale of pictures, not services, and applying the Uniform Commercial Code, he interpreted the consents and found them void because they were "unconscionable" (see Uniform Commercial Code, secs. 2-102,2-302). Plaintiff had not raised that issue before the trial court, however,nor did the parties present evidence on it and we have not considered it (seeUniform Commercial Code, sec. 2-302, subd [2]). Justice Carro dissented and voted to affirm the judgment of Trial Term. It was his view that the consents given in conformity with the statute constituted general releases and provided a complete defense to plaintiff's subsequent action.

The parties have filed cross appeals. Defendant requests reinstatement of the trial court's judgment. Plaintiff requests, in the alternative, that the order of the Appellate Division be modified by striking the limitation enjoining use only for purposes of advertising and trade, or that the order of the Appellate Division should be affirmed or, failing both of these, that a new trial be granted. Since the Appellate Division accepted the trial court's findings that the consents were valid and unrestricted as to time and use, we are presented with only a narrow issue of law concerning the legal effect to be given to the parent's consents.

Historically, New York common law did not recognize a cause of action for invasion of privacy (Arrington v New York Times Co., 55 NY2d 433; Roberson v Rochester Folding Box Co., 171 NY 538). In 1909, however, responding to the Roberson decision, the Legislature enacted sections 50 and 51 of the Civil Rights Law. Section 50 is penal and makes it a misdemeanor to use a living person's name, portrait or picture for advertising purposes without prior "written consent". Section 51 is remedial and creates a related civil cause of action on behalf of the injured party permitting relief by injunction or damages (see Arrington v New York Times Co., supra, at p 439; Flores v Mosler Safe Co., 7 NY2d 276, 280). Section 51 of the statute states that the prior "written consent" which will bar the civil action is to be as "above provided", referring to section 50, and section 50, in turn, provides that: "A person, firm or corporation that uses for advertising purposes, or for the purposes of trade, the name, portrait or picture of any living person without having first obtained the written consent of such person, or if a minor of his or her parent or guardian, is guilty of a misdemeanor" (emphasis added).

Thus, whereas in Roberson, the infant plaintiff had no cause of action against the advertiser under the common law for using her pictures, the new statute gives a cause of action to those similarly situated unless they have executed a consent or release in writing to the advertiser before use of the photographs. The statute acts to restrict an advertiser's prior unrestrained common-law right to use another's photograph until written consent is obtained. Once written consent is obtained, however, the photograph may be published as permitted by its terms (see Welch v Mr. Christmas, 57 NY2d 143).

Concededly, at common law an infant could disaffirm his written consent (see Joseph v Schatzkin, 259 NY 241; Casey v Kastel, 237 NY 305) or, for that matter, a consent executed by another on his or her behalf (see Lee v Silver, 262 App Div 149, affd 287 NY 575; Goldfinger v Doherty, 153 Misc 826, affd 244 App Div 779; Aborn v Janis, 62

Misc 95, affd 122 App Div 893). Notwithstanding these rules, it is clear that the Legislature may abrogate an infant's common-law right to disaffirm (see, e.g., General Obligations Law, sec. 3-101, subd 3; sec. 3-102, subd 1; sec. 3-103; Education Law, sec. 281; Insurance Law, sec. 145) or, conversely, it may confer upon infants the right to make binding contracts (see Matter of T.W.C., 38 NY2d 128, 130 [Domestic Relations Law, sec. 115-b]; Hamm v Prudential Ins. Co. of Amer., 137 App Div 504[Insurance Law, sec. 145, formerly sec. 55]; Matter of Presler, 171 Misc 559). Where a statute expressly permits a certain class of agreements to be made by infants, that settles the question and makes the agreement valid and enforceable. That is precisely what happened here. The Legislature, by adopting section 51, created a new cause of action and it provided in the statute itself the method for obtaining an infant's consent to avoid liability. Construing the statute strictly, as we must since it is in derogation of the common law (see McKinney's Cons Laws of NY, Book 1, Statutes, sec. 301, subd b), the parent's consent is binding on the infant and no words prohibiting disaffirmance are necessary to effectuate the legislative intent. Inasmuch as the consents in this case complied with the statutory requirements, they were valid and may not be disaffirmed (see Matter of T.W.C., supra).

Nor do we believe that the consents may be considered void because the parties failed to comply with the provisions of section 3-105 of the General Obligations Law requiring prior court approval of infants' contracts. By its terms, section 3-105 applies only to performing artists, such as actors, musicians, dancers and professional athletes moreover, it is apparent by comparing other statutes with it that the Legislature knowingly has differentiated between child performers and child models. Thus, section 3229 (formerly sec. 3216-c) of the Education Law, which applies to "Child performers", is referred to in section 3-105 (subd 2, par a) of the General Obligations Law but section 3230 of the Education Law, which applies to child models, is not. Child models are also recognized as a separate work classification in section 172 (subd 2, par f) of the Labor Law. Furthermore, section 3-105 was not designed to expand the rights of infants to disaffirm their contracts, as the concurring Justice at the Appellate Division would apply it, but to provide assurance to those required to deal with infants that the infants would not later disaffirm executory contracts to the adult contracting party's disadvantage (see Matter of Prinze [Jonas], 38 NY2d 570, 575). Sections 50 and 51 as we interpret them serve the same purpose, to bring certainty to an important industry which necessarily uses minors for its work. This same need for certainty was the impetus behind not only section 3-105 but the various other sections of the General Obligations Law which prohibit disaffirmance of an infant's contract.

Realistically, the procedures of prior court approval set forth in section 3-105, while entirely appropriate and necessary for performing artists and professional athletes, are impractical for a child model who, whether employed regularly or sporadically, works from session to session, sometimes for many different photographers. Moreover, they work for fees which are relatively modest when compared to those received by actors or professional athletes who may be employed by one employer at considerably greater remuneration for a statutorily permissible three-year term. Indeed, the fee in this case was $ 450, hardly sufficient to warrant the elaborate court proceedings required by section 3-105 or to necessitate a court's determination of what part should be set aside and preserved for the infant's future needs. Nor do we think court approval necessary under the circumstances existing in the normal child model's career. Given the nature of the employment, it is entirely reasonable for the Legislature to substitute the parents' judgment and approval of what is best for their child for that of a court.

It should be noted that plaintiff did not contend that the photographs were obscene or pornographic. Her only complaint was that she was embarrassed because "they [the photographs] are not me now." The trial court specifically found that the photographs were not pornographic and it enjoined use of them in pornographic publications. Thus, there is no need to discuss the unenforceability of certain contracts which violate public policy (see, e.g., Penal Law, @ 235.00 et seq.) or to equate an infant's common-law right to disaffirm with that principle, as the dissent apparently does.

Finally, it is claimed that the application of the statute as we interpret it may result in unanticipated and untoward consequences. If that be so, there is an obvious remedy. A parent who wishes to limit the publicity and exposure of her child need only limit the use authorized in the consent, for a defendant's immunity from a claim for invasion of privacy is no broader than the consent executed to him (see Welch v Mr. Christmas, 57 NY2d 143, supra; Adrian v Unterman, 281 App Div 81, affd 306 NY 771).

The order of the Appellate Division should be modified by striking the further injunction against use of the photographs for uses of advertising and trade, and as so modified, the order should be affirmed.

DISSENT: Since I believe that the interests of society and this State in protecting its children must be placed above any concern for trade or commercialism, I am compelled to dissent. The State has the right and indeed the obligation to afford extraordinary protection to minors.

At the outset, it should be made clear that this case does not involve the undoing of a written consent given by a mother to invade her infant daughter's privacy so as to affect prior benefits derived by a person relying on the validity of the consent pursuant to sections 50 and 51 of the Civil Rights Law. Rather, what is involved is the right of an infant, now 17 years of age, to disaffirm her mother's consent with respect to future use of a nude photograph taken of her at age 10.

The majority holds, as a matter of law, not only in this case but as to all present and future consents executed by parents on behalf of children pursuant to sections 50 and 51 of the Civil Rights Law, that once a parent consents to the invasion of privacy of a child, the child is forever bound by that consent and may never disaffirm the continued invasion of his or her privacy, even where the continued invasion of the child's privacy may cause the child enormous embarrassment, distress and humiliation.

I find this difficult to accept as a rational rule of law, particularly so when one considers that it has long been the rule in this State that a minor enjoys an almost absolute right to disaffirm a contract entered into either by the minor or by the minor's parent on behalf of the minor (Sternlieb v Normandie Nat. Securities Corp., 263 NY 245; Joseph v Schatzkin, 259 NY 241; International Text Book Co. v Connelly, 206 NY 188; Rice v Butler, 160 NY 578; Sparman v Keim, 83 NY 245; Green v Green, 69 NY 553) and the statute in question does not in any manner abrogate this salutary right.

This right has been upheld despite the fact that the minor held himself out to be an adult (Sternlieb v Normandie Nat. Securities Corp., supra) or that a parent also attempted to contractually bind the minor (Kaufman v American Youth Hostels, 13 Misc 2d 8, mod on other grounds 6 AD2d 223, mod and certified question answered in negative 5 NY2d 1016). Significantly, whether or not the minor can restore the other contracting party to the position he was in prior to entering the contract is pertinent only to the extent that the minor, by disaffirming the contract, cannot put himself into a better position than he was in before entering the contract. (Sternlieb v Normandie Nat. Securities Corp., supra; Rice v Butler, supra.) In the past, this court has noted that those who contract with minors do so at their own peril. (Joseph v Schatzkin, supra, at p 243.)

Understandably, such a broad right has evolved as a result of the State's policy to provide children with as much protection as possible against being taken advantage of or exploited by adults. "The right to rescind is a legal right established for the protection of the infant" (Green v Green, supra, at p 556). This right is founded in the legal concept that an infant is incapable of contracting because he does not understand the scope of his rights and he cannot appreciate the consequences and ramifications of his decisions. Furthermore, it is feared that as an infant he may well be under the complete influence of an adult or may be unable to act in any manner which would allow him to defend his rights and interests. (28 NY Jur, Infants, sec. 3, pp 221-222.) Allowing a minor the right to disaffirm a contract is merely one way the common law developed to resolve those inequities and afford children the protection they require to compensate for their immaturity.

Can there be any question that the State has a compelling interest in protecting children? Indeed, the most priceless possessions we have in the Nation are our children. Recognizing this compelling interest in children, the State has assumed the role of parens patriae, undertaking with that role the responsibility of protecting children from their own inexperience. Acting in that capacity, the State has put the interests of minors above that of adults, organizations or businesses. (Rice v Butler, supra; Kaufman v American Youth Hostels, supra; Sternlieb v Normandie Nat. Securities Corp., supra.) The broad right given a minor to disaffirm a contract is, of course, an obvious example of the State's attempt to afford an infant protection against exploitation by adults. (28 NY Jur, Infants, op. cit.) Thus, I am persuaded that, in this case, 17-year-old Brooke Shields should be afforded the right to disaffirm her mother's consent to use a photograph of her in the nude, taken when she was 10 years old, unless it can be said, as the majority holds, that the Legislature intended to abrogate that right when it enacted sections 50 and 51 of the Civil Rights Law.

The legislative history of this statute enacted in the early 1900's is understandably scarce. The case law prior to its passage, however, indicates that a minor's right to disaffirm a contract under the common law was well established at that time. Additionally, it is well accepted that this statute was enacted in response to this court's decision in Roberson v Rochester Folding Box Co. (171 NY 538; see, also, Arrington v New York Times Co., 55 NY2d 433, 439) in which the court held that a minor had no recourse against an entrepreneur who made commercial use out of her picture without her consent. Apparently, in order to alleviate litigation over whether or not consent had been given, the Legislature required that such consent be in writing and, if the person was a minor, that the parent sign the consent form. There is no indication that by requiring consent from the minor's parents, the Legislature intended in any way to abrogate that minor's right to disaffirm a contract at some future date. Indeed, the requirement of parental consent, like the broad right to disaffirm a contract, was granted in order to afford the minor as much protection against exploitation as possible. The assumption, of course, was that a parent would protect the child's interests. But if that assumption proves invalid, as may well be the case if a minor upon reaching the age of maturity realizes that the parent, too, has been exploiting him or her or had failed to adequately guard his or her interest by giving consent for pictures which caused humiliation, embarrassment and distress, then the child should be able to cure the problem by disaffirming the parent's consent. To say, as does the majority, that the mother could have limited her consent avoids the issue. If the parent has failed to put any restrictions on the consent, as occurred in this case, and has thus failed to protect the child's future interests, I see no reason why the child must continue to bear the burden imposed by her mother's bad judgment. This means the child is forever bound by its parent's decisions, even if those decisions turn out to have been exploitative of the child and detrimental to the child's best interests.

Furthermore, nothing compels the majority's conclusion that the right to disaffirm a contract was eliminated when the Legislature created a new cause of action for invasion of privacy merely because that statute provided safeguards for the child's privacy by giving the parent the right to grant or withhold consent. When both rights are viewed, as I believe they must be, as protection for the child, logic and policy compels the conclusion that the two rights should exist coextensively. The requirement that a parent consent before the child's privacy can be invaded by commercial interests establishes the parent as the first guardian of the child's interest. But the State retains its long-standing role of parens patriae so that if the parent fails to protect the child's interests, the State will intervene and do so. One means of doing so is to allow the child to exercise its right to disaffirm if the child concludes that its parent improvidently consented to the invasion of the child's privacy interests. Given the strong policy concern of the State in the child's best interests, I can only conclude that the Legislature did not intend to abrogate the child's common-law right to disaffirm a contract when it required, by statute, the additional protection of written, parental consent prior to any commercial use of the child's image.

This conclusion is further supported by other statutes in which the Legislature has clearly abrogated the infant's right to disaffirm a contract in those situations in which it has determined that the damage incurred by the minor will be minimal and the cost to the contracting party or society would be great. Invariably, these are contractual situations in which the minor has incurred a contractual obligation in order to receive a benefit which cannot be deemed anything other than a benefit. For example, section 281 of the Education Law negates a minor's right to disaffirm a contract when that contract afforded him a student loan to pursue an advanced education. (See, also, General Obligations Law, sec. 3-103.) No one can argue that the contract was anything other than beneficial to the minor. Such legislation was endorsed by the Law Revision Commission on the basis of a legislative finding "that the type of contract involved is clearly for the benefit of the infant". (1961 Report of NY Law Rev Comm, pp 269, 275, citing Touster, Contracts Relating to the Services of Talented Minors and the Treatment of Their Earnings Therefrom.)

Two factors distinguish sections 50 and 51 of the Civil Rights Law from those statutory provisions which do, in certain contexts, abolish the minor's right to disaffirm a contract. The first is that in all cases when the Legislature has intended to do so, they have made their intention clear by specific language which directly refers to the infant's common-law right. The absence of any reference in the Civil Rights Law to the minor's right to disaffirm a contract, especially when it is clear that the right to disaffirm was well established, indicates that the Legislature did not intend to affect that right. Secondly, unlike the other kinds of contracts which the Legislature has designated as immune from the minor's right to disaffirm, it cannot be said that a contract releasing all rights to photographs or even limited rights to those pictures is necessarily beneficial to the infant. This is even more true when the pictures, as in this case, are of the variety which can be exploited in the future or used in publications of questionable taste.

I do not believe that the Legislature's intent in enacting sections 50 and 51 of the Civil Rights Law was to elevate the interests of business and commercialism above the State's interest in protecting its children. Since this statute was enacted in response to this court's decision in Roberson v Rochester Folding Box Co. (supra), which denied an infant plaintiff any recovery for the invasion of her privacy by a commercial enterprise in using her picture without her consent, it would seem to me that the legislative intent was to expand individual protections, rather than to afford protection to commercial enterprises.

The fact that when an infant disaffirms a contract there may be harsh results to the person or commercial enterprise attempting to exploit the child has never caused the courts to alter the scope of the protection that right affords the child. The overriding interest of society in protecting its children has long been held to outweigh the interests of merchants who attempt to contract with children. (Sternlieb v Normandie Nat. Securities Corp., supra, at p 250.)

In those situations in which the Legislature has decided that business ventures need additional protection, it has done so not merely by abolishing the infant's right to disaffirm, but, rather, by providing alternative protection. Section 3-105 of the General Obligations Law provides for judicial approval of contracts for the services of child performers or professional athletes. It is clear that the statute protects not only the business interests which are investing in and profiting from the child's talents, but also the child. For instance, paragraph d of subdivision 2 generally restricts such contracts to a three-year period and paragraph e of subdivision 2 provides that even after approving a contract of a child performer, the court may, if it finds that the child's well-being is in any way being impaired by its performance under the contract, revoke or modify the contract so as to protect the child. Similarly, it provides for supervision by the court of the child's earnings to assure that the child will benefit from his labors. The clear intent of such provisions is to protect the child against any exploitation. The failure of the Legislature to cover child models in this provision indicates to me that they intended child models to retain the protections afforded by the common-law right to disaffirm a contract. It is unfortunate that by virtue of the majority's interpretation of the Civil Rights Law those children may not in the future be afforded protection against exploitation by their own parents.

The sole issue on appeal in this chancery proceeding is whether the trial court correctly ruled that a grantor possessed the mental capacity to execute a valid deed.

On September 19, 1986, Edith Hatchel, the grantor, a widow 72 years of age, executed a deed to appellee Resort Developments, the grantee, conveying four parcels of real estate located in the City of Virginia Beach for a total sales price of $ 70,000. On November 10, 1986, the court below appointed Ardelle Grimes, a niece of the grantor, as guardian for the person and estate of Hatchel. The court found, following an October 17, 1986 hearing on the guardianship petition filed by the City Department of Social Services, that Hatchel "is incapacitated by reason of mental illness."

In January 1987, the guardian filed the instant bill of complaint seeking to have the deed "set aside and declared void and invalid." The sole ground of relief was that the grantor "because of her advanced age and impaired health was not mentally able to understand the nature of the deed she signed." The guardian did not allege that the grantor had been subjected to either undue influence or constructive fraud.

Subsequently, the chancellor referred the matter to a commissioner in chancery, who held a hearing in September 1987. On conflicting evidence, the commissioner found the guardian had failed to prove that the grantor was incompetent at the time she signed the deed and that she was mentally unable to understand the nature of the instrument.

The guardian filed exceptions to the report, which the trial court overruled after considering argument of counsel. The chancellor confirmed the report, noting that the court "carefully reviewed and weighed the evidence presented, and reviewed and examined the conclusions of said Commissioner." We awarded the guardian this appeal from the March 1988 final decree entered in favor of the grantee. Later, the grantor died; upon suggestion of the death, we ordered the executor of Hatchel's estate to be substituted as the appellant in this proceeding. See Code sec. 8.01-20.

In a suit to invalidate a deed upon the ground of mental incapacity, the applicable law is settled. Every person is presumed to be of sound mind, and the burden is upon the party who alleges to the contrary to establish such charge. Howard v. Howard, 112 Va. 566, 568, 72 S.E. 133, 133 (1911). The test for determining whether one lacks sufficient capacity to become bound absolutely by deed or contract is whether, at the time the instrument was executed, the grantor possessed sufficient mental capacity to understand the nature of the transaction and to agree to its provisions. Lohman v. Sherwood, 181 Va. 594, 607, 26 S.E.2d 74, 79-80 (1943). Mental ability varies from one individual to another; therefore, no specific degree of mental acuteness is to be prescribed as the measure of one's capacity to execute a deed. McGrue v. Brownfield, 202 Va. 418, 425, 117 S.E.2d 701, 706 (1961). And, when mental capacity is in issue, the outcome of every case must depend mainly on the facts surrounding the execution of the deed in question. Id. at 424, 117 S.E.2d at 706. Hence, the testimony of witnesses who were present when the instrument was executed is entitled to greater weight than the testimony of those witnesses not present. Howard, 112 Va. at 570, 72 S.E. at 134.

In the present case, a detailed recitation of the conflicting evidence is unnecessary. Under established principles of appellate review, the judgment below is presumed to be correct, especially where, as here, the finding of the commissioner who heard the testimony ore tenus has been confirmed by the chancellor. As we shall demonstrate, the record fully supports the commissioner's finding.

In her attempt to prove the grantor's incapacity, the guardian presented evidence that during periods before and after execution of the deed Hatchel was disoriented, confused, and unable to understand any written instrument. According to the testimony, the grantor's mental condition had begun deteriorating shortly before her retirement in 1984 from city employment. Witnesses related instances of bizarre conduct by the grantor including a time in 1985 when she travelled to Norfolk for a party and later was found near Richmond when she intended to return to her home in Virginia Beach.

A number of witnesses for the guardian opined that the grantor was incapable of understanding or agreeing to the provisions of a deed in September 1986. For example, a psychologist, who had evaluated the grantor in connection with the guardianship proceeding, testified that based on available information, including a conversation with the grantor on October 13, 1986, "I don't think there's any way this lady could have understood what she was doing" at the time the deed was executed.

None of the guardian's witnesses who testified about the grantor's incapacity were present at the closing of the land transaction when the deed was executed, except the grantor. During her testimony before the commissioner in September 1987, a year after the closing, the grantor made generally nonsensical statements.

In contrast to the evidence offered on behalf of the guardian, the grantee presented the testimony of three persons who attended the closing, held in the law office of the grantee's attorney. Present at the closing were the grantor, a male friend who lived in her home, the grantor's attorney, the grantee's attorney, and the real estate agent who negotiated the transaction for the grantee. According to that testimony, every document considered or executed during the closing was explained in detail to the grantor, and she appeared to understand the entire transaction and the associated papers, including the deed.

The grantor's attorney testified that he met his client on at least two occasions prior to closing and that her mental awareness during these meetings was "good." At the time of closing, the attorney testified, the grantor "knew what was going on" and understood that she was conveying her property in accordance with her desires. The grantee's attorney testified that during the closing, which lasted about 45 minutes to an hour, there was "no doubt" in his mind that the grantor "knew what was going on and was cognizant of what she was doing." The attorney testified that the whole transaction was absolutely explained to a dead certainty" and that she "definitely" appeared to understand the explanation. The commissioner reported: "Both of the attorneys present at the settlement enjoy impeccable reputations."

The real estate agent had dealt with the grantor for months before she executed the contract of sale for the property in July 1986. He testified that, at closing, she understood she was signing a deed to property which included her home and that she was mentally capable of understanding the nature of her act.

In his appellate argument, the executor treats the case as if the guardian had sought relief upon the ground of undue influence. As we have said, only lack of mental capacity was pled, a matter conceded during argument before the chancellor. Persisting on appeal to discuss undue influence, however, the executor focuses on one of the elements of such a claim, i.e. a showing of the grantor's "great weakness of mind," see Martin v. Phillips, 235 Va. 523, 527, 369 S.E.2d 397, 399 (1988). Specifically, the executor contends, he should prevail on a claim of incapacity because the trial court found, both from the bench and in the final decree, that the grantor "had great weakness of mind during the period when the subject contract and deed wereexecuted." We reject such a contention.

Mental weakness alone will not invalidate an instrument because courts do not engage in measuring "the size of peoples' understanding or capacities." Lohman, 181 Va. at 607, 26 S.E.2d at 80. Therefore, in the context of a suit like this based solely on lack of mental capacity to execute a deed, proof of "great weakness of mind" is insufficient to establish mental incapacity. In other words, a person may have great weakness of mind yet may possess sufficient mental capacity to understand the nature of the transaction and to assent to the provisions of the challenged instrument. Thus, the trial court's finding of "great weakness of mind" is not inconsistent with its confirmation of the commissioner's report.

For these reasons, we hold that the trial court did not err in refusing to invalidate the deed in question. Therefore, the trial court's final decree will be Affirmed.

CRYSCO OILFIELD SERVICES, INC. v. HUTCHISON-HAYES INTERNATIONAL, INC.
913 F.2d 850 10th Cir. 1990)

After examining the briefs and appellate record, this panel has determined unanimously that oral argument would not materially assist the determination of this appeal. See Fed. R. App. P. 34(a). 10th Cir. R. 34.1.9. The case is therefore ordered submitted without oral argument.

I. Facts

Defendant supplied plaintiff with machinery known as shale shakers for use in the oil well servicing business. The shale shakers did not work properly. Plaintiff sued defendant for breach of an implied warranty of fitness for a particular purpose and for violation of the Oklahoma Consumer Protection Act, 15 Okla. Stat. Secd. 752-63 (1981).

At trial, defendant moved for a directed verdict on the implied warranty claim after plaintiff had presented its case in chief. The district court denied the motion. On September 22, 1989, the jury returned a verdict in favor of plaintiff on the implied warranty claim. Defendant now appeals the trial court's entry of judgment on the jury's verdict. Defendant claims that the trial court wrongfully denied its motion for a directed verdict at trial. We believe that a directed verdict was appropriate. Therefore, we reverse the case and remand to the district court.

II. Discussion

In order to reverse the trial court's decision on a motion for directed verdict we must find that "the evidence points but one way and is susceptible to no reasonable inferences supporting the party [opposing the motion]; we must construe the evidence and inferences most favorably to the nonmoving party." Zimmerman v. First Federal Sav. & Loan Ass'n., 848 F.2d 1047, 1051 (10th Cir. 1988). We believe that this high standard is met in this case. The facts are essentially undisputed by the parties. The real issue is whether the trial court correctly interpreted the law in application to these facts. We believe that the trial court incorrectly interpreted the law.

Plaintiff's claim for an implied warranty of fitness for particular purpose is based on the Oklahoma statute adopting section 2-315 of the Uniform Commercial Code.

Where the seller at the time of contracting has reason to know any particular purpose for which the goods are required and that the buyer is relying on the seller's skill or judgment to select or furnish suitable goods, there is unless excluded or modified under the next section an implied warranty that the goods shall be fit for such purpose.

12A Okla. Stat. Sec. 2-315 (1981). Oklahoma's adoption of the exact language of the UCC creates two separate requirements for a claim to arise under this section. First, the seller must know that the goods will be used for a "particular purpose." Second, the buyer must rely on the skill or judgment of the seller in selecting suitable goods. See American Fertilizer Specialists, Inc. v. Wood, 635 P.2d 592, 595 (Okla. 1981); Collins Radio Co. of Dallas v. Bell, 623 P.2d 1039, 1054 (Ct. App. Okla. 1980); Jackson v. Glasgow, 622 P.2d 1088, 1090 (Ct. App. Okla. 1980). We do not reach the second requirement because we hold that plaintiff did not use the shale shakers for a "particular purpose" as required by section 2-315.

The record indicates that the shale shakers were manufactured to be used in oil fields in precisely the manner used by plaintiff. We hold that the use of a good in the ordinary manner for which the good was manufactured does not satisfy section 2-315's requirement that the good be used for a "particular purpose." In a case in which we interpreted section 2-315, as adopted by Colorado, we pointed out that "the statute distinguishes between an ordinary purpose giving rise to an implied warranty of merchantability and a particular purpose giving rise to an implied warranty of fitness for a particular purpose." Weir v. Federal Ins. Co., 811 F.2d 1387, 1393 (10th Cir. 1987). In Weir, the plaintiffs purchased a clothes dryer and used it for drying clothes. We held:

The jury in the present case was instructed that drying clothes could serve as the particular purpose that the Weirs had in mind in selecting the clothes dryer. It is obvious, however, that drying clothes is only the ordinary purpose of a clothes dryer. . . . Thus, the district judge erred in instructing the jury that drying clothes could be the "particular purpose" necessary to establish an implied warranty of fitness for a particular purpose.

Id. at 1393.

Thus, we have interpreted UCC section 2-315 to require a particular purpose as opposed to any ordinary purpose. This interpretation is supported by many other courts and by the leading commentators in this field. As White and Summers explain:

Recently some courts have held that the 2-315 warranty as to fitness for a particular purpose may arise when the buyer's "specific use" is the same as the "general use" to which the goods under contract are usually put. We are wary of such cases. They apparently enlarge the scope of the 2-315 warranty beyond the intent of the drafters.

J. White & R. Summers, Uniform Commercial Code sec. 9-10 at 481 n.1 (3d ed. 1988) (citations omitted). White and Summers then go on to cite a string of cases adopting the view that section 2-315 does not apply where the buyer's "specific use" coincides with the "general use" of the goods. Id. We point out two cases clearly adopting this view. See Intern. Petrol. Serv., Inc. v. S & N Well Serv., 230 Kan. 452, 639 P.2d 29, 37 (1982); Duford v. Sears, Roebuck and Co., 833 F.2d 407, 413 (1st Cir. 1987).

Having reviewed the Oklahoma cases in this area, we conclude that Oklahoma follows the position discussed above. For example, in American Fertilizer Specialists, Inc. v. Wood, 635 P.2d 592 (Okla. 1981), the Supreme Court of Oklahoma considered a case involving a sale of fertilizer. In Wood, the seller contacted the buyer and suggested a new fertilizer mix for use on the buyer's pasture land. When the fertilizer failed to work, the buyer sued asserting implied warranties of merchantability and fitness for particular purpose. See Wood, 635 P.2d at 594-95.

In considering the buyer's warranty claims, the Wood court clearly recognized a distinction between the two implied warranties. Indeed, the court quoted the language of the comment to UCC section 2-315 regarding what is a "particular purpose." See id. at 595 n. 8. Having considered carefully the UCC language, the court pointed out that the seller knew of the particular purpose for the fertilizer and that the buyer had relied on the seller's skill in selecting a proper mix. Id. at 595. Accordingly, the court held that under those facts "there was competent evidence reasonably tending to support the trial court's conclusion, and to support the judgment in favor of [the buyer] on the ground of breach of implied warranty under both sec. 2-314 and sec. 2-315 of 12A O.S. 1971." Id. at 594.

Based on its decision in Wood, we believe the Oklahoma courts follow our interpretation of section 2-315. The court focused specifically on the fact that the seller was aware of the particular purpose for which the fertilizer would be used. We do not believe such evidence would have been critical unless the court was following our interpretation of section 2-315.

We acknowledge the similarity between our case and the facts of Wood. One critical distinction, however, mandates a different result in this case. Unlike the fertilizer in Wood, which can have many formulations for various purposes, the shale shakers involved here have only one possible use. Consequently, we must conclude that while the fertilizer involved in Wood was for a particular use, the shale shakers here were purchased for their ordinary use.

Plaintiff cites two additional Oklahoma cases that are also distinguishable. In Larrance Tank Corp. v. Burrough, 476 P.2d 346 (Okla. 1970), the defendant provided underground tanks to plaintiff for the storage of gas. The court upheld the plaintiff's subsequent claim under section 2-315. However, unlike this case, it is likely that the tanks could have been used for a variety of purposes and that the defendant was well aware that the tanks would be used for the particular purpose of holding gas. Moreover, the case does not clearly adopt an interpretation of section 2-315 contrary to our own reading of Wood. Plaintiff also cites Old Albany Estates v. Highland Carpet Mills, 604 P.2d 849 (Okla. 1980). In Old Albany the defendant provided carpet to the plaintiff knowing that it would be used in an apartment building. When the carpet wore out prematurely, the plaintiff sued under section 2-315. The Oklahoma Supreme Court held that the plaintiff was entitled to damages under section 2-315. In Old Albany the defendant knew that a higher grade of carpet was necessary because of the plaintiff's particular use. As discussed above, however, the shale shakers in this case were not used in an unusual or "particular" manner.

III. Conclusion

We interpret Oklahoma's adoption of section 2-315 of the UCC in conformity with our prior interpretation of the same section adopted in Colorado. We hold that section 2-315 requires a particular purpose or use separate from the general or ordinary use of the product. The record before us indicates that plaintiff used the shale shakers in the normal, general manner that the shakers were typically used. We hold that such use does not fall under section 2-315. Thus, plaintiff has made no claim under section 2-315, and the trial court's failure to grant a directed verdict must be reversed.

We REVERSE the trial court's judgment in this case and REMAND to the district court for further proceedings consistent with this opinion.